Olive Manuel
One in Ten

*Olive, circa 1957, with her first child,
(Dorothy) Jane*

"One in Ten"
Copyright © 2009 by Olive A. Manuel

First published 2009 by Lulu.com

All rights reserved. No part of this publication may be reproduced, stored in a retrieval system or transmitted in any form or by any means without the prior written permission of the author, nor be otherwise circulated in any form of binding or cover other than that in which it is published and without a similar condition being imposed on the subsequent purchaser.

Body copy typeset in Lapidary 9pt
Project graphic design & page make-up by John P. Manuel

Further copies of this book may be purchased from:
http://www.lulu.com/content/paperback-book/one-in-ten/7567274

or via http://honorarygreek.blogspot.com

1st edition • 09.09

Front cover photo of the author, circa 1950

ISBN:

978-1-4452-0041-5

Olive Manuel (née Greensides) was born in November 1927 in Bath, England. Her parents Francis (Frank) and Lilian (Lil) had thirteen children in total, but three were lost at birth, leaving ten who survived.

This fascinating, albeit brief, snapshot of what it was like to be a teenager just before and during the Second World War is both heartwarming and educational. It vividly brings to life the kind of conditions which a family at the time would have had to contend with, whilst also revealing why Olive came through it all as a well-balanced individual, able to marry and successfully raise two children of her own.

The secret, which shines through in her writing, is her cheerful disposition, despite what life may have thrown against her at times. Anyone who knows her will readily agree that she is ever the optimist and is always quick with a smile.

Small wonder she is loved by all who know her.

Acknowledgements

I would especially like to thank my mum and dad for the wonderful childhood which they gave my sister Jane and I. We like to think that we didn't give our parents a day's bother or worry while we were growing up. *Several* maybe!

I hope this small book goes some way to showing my mum, Olive just how much she is loved.

I am indebted to Daniel Brown for his help in obtaining the images on pages 19, 20 & 37.
There were all obtained from:
http://www.bathintime.co.uk - Bath Central Library Collection

John Manuel

For my dear and very much missed late husband,
Kenneth Thomas Manuel
7th March 1929 - 16th January 2009

Olive A. Manuel

Olive Manuel

Part One

One In Ten

1.

What was it like being one of a large family, growing up before and during the Second World War? It was sometimes sad, often exciting, yet always our home was full of love. My mum had ten surviving children, and three more which were either still-born, or died shortly after birth. The children comprised of six boys and four girls. I was the one in the middle, number five in the birth order, born in November of 1927.

My father Francis was in the British Army when my parents first met. He'd run away from home in Beverley, Yorkshire to join up at 15, eventually becoming a Sergeant Major with the Somerset Light Infantry. He was a wonderful Dad and he loved both his wife and his children very much. I was told that most of us were "rounded", both at birth and during the early years, although I was the exception, the skinny one. I was very thin and was always being made fun of, but I just got used to it and eventually ignored most of it. I have to say it was never (well, almost never) with malicious intent, just "fun."

The street where we lived in my earliest memory was Northampton Buildings in Bath, which was then in the county of Somerset, England,

UK. It was made up of modest Georgian (though probably Victorian) terraced housing and was quite narrow, involved quite a steep incline and curved around at the top to create a cul-de-sac where we children could play in relative safety. Steep steps rose from the pavement to our front door, which had a wide brass step which my sister Betty (Elizabeth) and I took turns to clean as part of our assigned chores. All the kids had jobs assigned to them by our parents. My favourite was helping mum with the washing. I would turn the handle on the big old mangle and loved seeing the water being squeezed out of the garments and pouring into the galvanised bucket below. I had to be sure the bucket was properly positioned, or mum would swear a bit if the water missed and spilled on to the floor!

In winter time the milkman would climb our steps with his churn and pour our milk directly into a large jug. Whenever the weather was icy he would never let mum go down the steps in order to save him lugging the heavy churn up to the front door. I saw many a pint or two of milk go flying when he'd slip on the top step! I secretly thought he had a bit of a soft spot for our mother!

The ten Greensides children who lived (3 more died as stillbirths or at birth). Left to right:
Michael, Muriel (behind), Robert [Bobby] (in front), Peter, William [Bill], Nin [Lilian, also called "Bobby"], Christopher, Elizabeth [Betty] and Olive. Richard (Dick) may well have taken this photograph, as he's the only one of the ten not included. The oldest picture of him which Olive could find is the one added to the right, of Dick as a teenager.

One in Ten

2.

Once every fortnight Dad would take us fishing and he would always catch lots of sprats. We'd troop home with dad's successful catch and, once back in the kitchen, watch dad as he'd wash the fish, take off their heads and then put them in the oven. That evening we'd all sit around the wooden table with greasy mouths and fingers and feast on sprats on toast for our "tea." It was "lovely grub!" On Saturday afternoons dad would go and lay down for a couple of hours and all our neighbours knew when it was 4 o'clock as we'd come in from play time and Dad would make thick rounds of pastry, cook them, then cut them in half and fill them with margarine and Golden Syrup. All the children would be given one each; it was a great treat for us.

Every Friday we'd wait for Dad to come home from work, when we'd all stand in a line with hands held out to receive or weekly pocket money, one penny. You could make a penny go a long way on sweets in the late 1930's. A farthing for a stick of liquorice, another for a roll of toffee and a ha'penny worth (called a "*hae-puth*") of bullseyes would

One in Ten

see us all spent out. Those sweets would last us a whole two days though - it was heaven.

Of all the meals I would look forward to, Sunday breakfast was my absolute favourite. Dad would put the frying pan on the gas and pile it with chopped tomatoes, bacon and sausage. he'd then add hot water and some Oxo, then dip thick slices of bread in and we'd all have a piece with the tomatoes and sausage on top. That breakfast was sooo good! How I still miss those Sunday mornings even today, all these decades later.

When he left the Army, Dad got a job at the Admiralty in Bath. He began at the bottom packing cases and doing other manual work. He was nothing if not industrious though and worked his way up until he got a position behind a desk in the offices where he was popular with all the staff who knew him.

Olive Manuel

3.

In 1942, when I was still just fourteen, Bath was hit by the "Blitz." German bombers took off from airfields in Northern France and were over our city in just an hour and a half. Between the evening of Saturday 25th and early morning hours of Monday 27th April, the city was bombed heavily and sustained a great deal of damage and loss of life.

From 1940 onwards there had been spasmodic bomb droppings in the area, but nothing to match what was to come on those nights in 1942. In fact, there were no bombs dropped on Bath at all from April 1941 until the Blitz of 1942, which led to some adopting the attitude that Bath was "safe." In fact, since Bristol had been a major target for a while, some even ignored the sirens in Bath this time and lost their lives as a result. After the Bath Blitz we discovered that we'd lost our home and all our possessions. Everything, all gone.

We were left with only what we stood up in as we'd had to leave home and go to the large air raid shelter in Queen Square. We spent the entire night in that shelter and I still see vividly in my mind's eye the scene that greeted us when we emerged the following day. The Francis Hotel, which occupied (and still does) the entire one side of the square had taken a direct hit.

I actually ran up and out of the shelter before I was told to and was greeted by the sight of bodies everywhere, or so it seemed to me, a fourteen year old girl. What sticks in my mind is the fact that I saw not simply bodies, but parts of bodies laying on the grass in the centre of the square. We were instructed to go to nearby Victoria Park and wait there. My elder brother Chris was home on leave, so he and our Dad went off to make the ten minute walk to Northampton Buildings to see if the house was OK. They returned about half an hour later, the both of them in tears.

"There's nothing left," they said, "Nothing at all. It's all gone." Our home had taken a direct hit and so, as I mentioned before, we were left with nothing but what we had with us, which was very little.

But we were alive.

We then walked about three miles, I can't remember why or where to, and were given some bread and jam, plus a little milk for my baby brother, who was then just six months old. We all felt shattered and totally helpless. We were then told to go to a Church Hall, I think it was St. Swithins in the Walcot area, where, when our names were called, we were to board a bus and be evacuated to somewhere in the countryside outside of the city.

After some difficulty we found the hall and joined a throng, all of whom were waiting. We waited and waited and still our names weren't called. Finally, Dad had had enough and told us children:

"Listen now. The next bus that comes along, we all get on. Don't

Olive Manuel

"There's nothing left...it's all gone."
The area around Northampton Buildings on the morning after the raid of April 26-27 1942.

This is what I saw as I emerged from the Queen Square shelter. It's the Francis Hotel, which had taken a direct hit.

Olive Manuel

hesitate, don't dawdle. Just get on board, got it? Good!" Which we did. Whereupon an official-looking man approached dad and asked him his name, then said:

"I haven't called you yet and you shouldn't be on this bus!" to which Dad replied,

"Well on it we are and on it we're staying!" ...And stay aboard we did. The official, evidently facing humiliation at the thought of a family of such a size making a stand against him, acquiesced and we were soon on our way to the village of Timsbury, some eight miles or more outside of Bath, where we were installed in a local miners welfare hut. It was built of stone and had a corrugated iron roof. During the eight months that we lived in that hut we seemed like gypsies, cooking outside on a wood fire. We practically lived on stews, but we survived and, since we were the largest family there, were the last to leave.

It was whilst living there in Timsbury that my sister Muriel and I had a bit of an incident. It was a nice sunny day and so we decided we would put our camp beds outside and stretch out to read our books in the sunshine. We'd been out there for around half an hour when I looked up and said, "oh look, there's a cow by the gate." Muriel looked up and suddenly shouted, "That's not a cow, it's a BULL!!" Camp beds flying in all directions, books heading skywards, we shot indoors and slammed the door behind us. That bull charged across and butted the door with its horns, which gave us the shakes and no mistake. What were we going to do? Suppose the door gave way?

Fortunately for us, suddenly we heard a gruff voice shouting, "COME ON YER OLD ****?!" It was the farmer. What a relief. He'd apparently escaped from the next door field, the bull that is, not the farmer!

During all the months we spent at Timsbury, my father had to cycle the seven or eight miles to Bath and back for work every day and, by the time he got home at night he was really whacked out, but had to keep going for all our sakes. As I was fourteen I'd been due to have an interview for a job in a wool shop in Bath, but unfortunately that shop was bombed before I could start, so I eventually got a job at good old Woolworth's, where I stayed for the next eleven years and really enjoyed it.

Olive Manuel

4.

After almost nine months of virtual outdoor living in Timsbury, we were given a three-bedroomed house in Cork Terrace, Bath. This was just about large enough as two of my brothers and one of my sisters were in the forces and doing very well for themselves. That left seven of us, plus my parents, at home, so, though it was a tight squeeze, it felt really good to be in a proper house again. It was a house that we could make into a home. The owner of the house was about eighty years old at the time and he kept telling people, rather grumpily,

"I've got ten bloody kids coming here!"

His attitude soon mellowed, however, when, after getting to know mum and how many ration books she had, from which he could get a bit of help (butter, cheese, tea etc.), she and him struck up a friendship. I remember well too that an old lady lived next door and in her garden grew gooseberries, raspberries and a very fruitful apple tree. The problem was, she was the type that would prefer to let it all rot than give you any! Our landlord, the old man, would go every now and then to pick her fruit for her, but heaven only knows what she did with it.

So he'd surreptitiously chuck handfuls of whatever he was picking at the time over the fence into our garden, where eager hands were waiting for the illicit harvest! We would soon be in the kitchen watching, mouths watering, as Dad made pastry with which he'd fashion wonderful fruit pies. With custard too, what a treat!

About this time my youngest sibling, my brother Bobby, was only about a year old when my elder sister, "Nin", told me that mum was pregnant again. I was stunned, as by now mum was forty seven. When she was seven months I remember waking up one morning to the sound of a lot of running about. Then I heard the midwife calling for hot water etc. and for Dad to make some cocoa. Mum delivered all of her children at home, except for her first, my brother Bill. My poor Dad would pace up and down muttering to himself, but this time the baby was stillborn, a beautiful little girl. It was a traumatic time as, although we were overcrowded, we would have loved that child.

In the years that followed we had sad times, happy times, but most of all - together times. When I was married, in 1949, my husband Ken and I would visit Mum and Dad and dad would relate his war experiences. he'd had a rough time, but how lucky we were that he came home. If he'd not survived to come home on leave from time to time, it's a certainty that not a few of my siblings would not be here today.

Olive Manuel

Here now in 2009, there are still six of us living and so much more to tell, but maybe another time. It was often tough, but also often funny. It was frequently joyous, but sometimes melancholy. My young days were crammed, though, with love and I wouldn't have missed being one of ten for anything.

Part Two

A little more of the story

by Olive's son, John

Olive Manuel

1.

My Mum married my Dad, Kenneth Thomas Manuel in December 1949. They met through mutual friends as Olive's Brother Dick was courting Jean Godwin, whose brother Ivor was courting Olive's sister Muriel. Both couples eventually married. Ken was a friend of Ivor's and had sung in the Church choir with him when they were younger. In fact Ken would tell a story or two of their antics in that choir with a twinkle in his eye.

One such story concerned the time (around 1941) when Dad had a sore throat, largely due to his own making, or so he thought, as he and Ivor had been out late the previous night and then stayed up almost all night talking on a sleep-over. The choirmaster was a strict man and Dad had to sing a soprano solo in an important service the next evening. As they walked to the Church for the occasion Dad realised he'd never make the high notes. He and Ivor knew what the result would be if they scuppered the choirmaster's moment of glory so they worried over what they could do about the problem.

Dad had already tried spoonfuls of honey, but to no avail. Then Ivor hit on the solution.

"You stand up and do your solo, Ken," he said, "but as I'll be seated

One in Ten

next to you, I'll hit the high notes and you mime them. No one will ever know!"

Well the service went off without a hitch, though Dad used to say he saw a spark in the old man's eyes as they changed out of their vestments afterwards.

But he never said a word about it.

Little did Dad know at the time, but the problem hadn't been their previous night's escapade. His voice was beginning to break and his days as a choirboy were drawing to a close as he was growing up.

2.

Ken's story is itself a novel in the making. He first met his father when he was fourteen years old, having been raised in Bath by his diminutive grandmother, Granny Mills, all on her own. She'd been already in her sixties when she took him on as a babe in arms, a matter in which she didn't have much choice.

Almost a year and a half younger than Olive, Ken was born in March of 1929 to Thomas and Dorothy Manuel, residents of Southampton. Dorothy hailed from Bath and I never found out how they'd first met. She breast-fed her baby son Kenneth and, when he was only six months old, was committed to Wells mental assylum, as such places were called in those times. The story went that Ken had "bitten the nipple" while feeding and caused his mother to suffer "milk fever," an illness which produces mental problems, from which the sufferer may never recover. Nowadays I am convinced they would have a much more accurate and likely diagnosis. In those times however, it seems this was the given wisdom.

His mother incapacitated indefinitely, his father Thomas took the young boy Kenneth to Bath and presented him to his maternal grandmother saying, "You'll have to raise the boy. I can't deal with it."

Granny Mills was five foot nothing but took the young child in and gave him all the love she could. She provided for him and he lacked nothing that someone in their station in life could have expected. I often asked Dad whether he felt deprived, not having two regular parents at home. Did he have problems with the other boys at school, for example. His reply was always, "No son. I never lacked anything and I had a good upbringing." He truly learned the meaning of the word *appreciation*.

It was when he was fourteen that his cousin Clarice (whom he'd call "aunty" as she was quite a lot older than him), who lived in Dorset, came to visit and told his grandmother that she'd like to take him on a day trip. They took the train to Southampton and, when Ken asked where they were going, her reply was:

"To meet someone you ought to know." Clarice always had a soft spot for her younger cousin and this was one of her ways of showing it. She was hoping, vainly as it turned out, that perhaps Thomas would see his son and feel a connection there; that he'd perhaps try and make efforts to heal the damage he'd caused by cutting himself off from the boy for thirteen and a half years.

Imagine the emotional turmoil in a fourteen year-old's heart when (in 1943) he was marched up to a strange front door in Shirley, Southampton, then, on seeing a stranger present himself at the open door, be told:

"Kenneth, kiss your father!"

Ken refused. Can you blame him?

Olive Manuel

*December 3rd, 1949, St John the Evangelist church,
Upper Bristol Road, Weston, Bath.*

One in Ten

The modest wedding party at Olive and Ken's wedding.

Left to right:
Ken's cousin Clarice, Olive's sister Muriel, Clarice's husband Charlie,
the bride & groom, Olives sister Betty, Olive's father Frank
and her mother Lilian

Olive Manuel

3.

A good indicator as to the kind of man Dad was becoming was the way - as a teenager - he took on the mantle of returning all the care that his grandmother had heaped upon him. He left school at fourteen to become an electrical apprentice. Though a gifted artist, who'd been told by his schoolmasters that he ought to go to art college, he realised that, since his grandmother was close to being bedridden, he needed to become the breadwinner. So he forsook his vocation and set about becoming a very good and conscientious electrician.

The courtship pursued by Ken and Olive revealed much about both their personalities. It was spent largely caring for Granny Mills, now totally bedridden in her final years. They'd snatch an hour or two together, then go home and while Ken cooked a meal for them all, Olive would give his grandmother a bed bath. In her final months they had to lift her on and off of the lavatory, wash and clean her and feed her. How she was repaid by that boy and his wife-to-be for all she'd sacrificed to give him a good start in life.

To return to the Bath blitz for a moment. It was while Olive and her family were living in Northampton Buildings, just up the hillside and the other side of Victoria Park from New King Street, where Ken was living with his grandmother, that the events of those two fateful nights in April 1942 occurred. Olive and Ken's paths hadn't yet crossed, but they were half a mile from each other when the bombs fell. One bomb blew a crater the entire width of the road outside Ken's home, destroying the Percy Boys' Club building in the process. Dad told of an ARP warden who was patrolling New King Street at the time and was never seen again after that night of August 27th 1942. They never even found his bicycle.

Olive and Ken married in 1949, Ken in the only suit he owned and Olive in a dress she'd made herself out of curtain material. Their first home was a modest one room flat in St. Marks Road, Widcombe. They began married life with a table, two chairs and a bed. Ken's auntie Annie (who we children would come to call "Granny Haines") was a strange woman and no mistake. To illustrate: she told Ken and Olive she'd like to buy them a wedding present. She settled on a roll of linoleum to go around the modestly sized rug they had in their room, to cover the bare floorboards. Dad was a little wary of this as he knew her to be very miserly. But she insisted and so it was delivered and laid. Some months after the wedding they paid her a visit, during which she said:

"When you're ready, I'll have the cash for that lino."

Dad used to say that he could have made an issue out of this. She had definitely told them it was a wedding present, but here she was asking to be paid for it. He and Mum knew full well that they'd never

New King Street, Bath the morning after the raid of April 26-27 1942. The photographer could almost have been standing on Granny Mills' doorstep.

have agreed to have it if they'd been expected to pay for it as it would have been a luxury they'd have done without. But they vowed that however long it took, they'd give her the money and never ask anything of her again. It took many months of scrimping, but she got her money, but lost the love and respect of two of her family for ever.

In August of 1951 Olive and Ken's first child was born. A girl they called Dorothy - after Ken's mother. But pretty soon, as she grew, she came to be known by her second name, Jane, and still is today. November 1953 saw the arrival of yours truly, making the Manuel family complete. A better childhood no one could have wished for. We weren't wealthy by any stretch of the imagination. But Both Jane and I never wanted for anything of value and had something which far too many children in these times fail to receive, the quality time and attention of two loving parents, people who truly appreciated the value of the important things.

But the story of Olive and Ken's family life is for another time.

Olive Manuel

John Manuel

...is the author of two light-hearted travel books about his experiences over three and a half decades of visiting Greece, leading up to his re-location with his wife to the island of Rhodes in 2005. The books are called FETA COMPLI! & MOUSSAKA TO MY EARS.

What have reviewers said about these books?

FETA COMPLI

"A really enjoyable read which made me laugh out loud several times. This is not just an entertaining travelogue but provides real insight into the Greek way of life and culture. I would highly recommend this author's first novel and it's a must read for anyone with an interest in anything GREEK!"

- http://www.lulu.com/content/paperback-book/feta-compli/733993

MOUSSAKA TO MY EARS

This is a lively and enchanting account of living on the island of Rhodes. ...In his first book, Feta Compli, John Manuel told a rambling story of how he came to fall in love with his wife, Yvonne-Maria, ...of how they drove all across Europe with their worldly goods to settle into half of a half-finished duplex on a raw building site. This sequel is a much more polished account, and even better — ornamented with pictures of some of the places and situations and characters which John and Yvonne encountered over the years. ...All in all, Moussaka to My Ears is a lovely evocation of a place and a people.

- http://www.bloggernews.net/121419

Both books are available from the following sources:

http://honorarygreek.blogspot.com
http://www.amazon.com/
http://stores.lulu.com/themanuels
or simply e-mail John: themanuels@rho.forthnet.gr

Printed in Great Britain
by Amazon